Important Dates

JANUARY

FEBRUARY

MARCH

APRIL

MAY

JUNE

JULY

AUGUST

SEPTEMBER

OCTOBER

NOVEMBER

DECEMBER

My Schedule

Time	Monday	Tuesday	Wednesday	Thursday	Friday

Important Information

My Goals for this year

Goal #1

Step #1

Step #2

Goal #2

Step #1

Step #2

Goal #3

Step #1

Step #2

What is something you want to learn or master this year?

My Passion Project

Step #1

Step #2

Step #3

	MONDAY	TUESDAY	WEDNESDAY
To Pack/bring	☐ ☐ ☐ ☐	☐ ☐ ☐ ☐	☐ ☐ ☐ ☐
Assignments Due	☐ ☐ ☐ ☐	☐ ☐ ☐ ☐	☐ ☐ ☐ ☐
Class Notes			
Homework Tasks	☐ ☐ ☐ ☐	☐ ☐ ☐ ☐	☐ ☐ ☐ ☐
Additional Notes			

THURSDAY

FRIDAY

NOTES

REMINDERS

NEXT WEEK

DOODLES

	MONDAY	TUESDAY	WEDNESDAY
To Pack/bring	☐ ☐ ☐ ☐	☐ ☐ ☐ ☐	☐ ☐ ☐ ☐
Assignments Due	☐ ☐ ☐ ☐	☐ ☐ ☐	☐ ☐ ☐
Class Notes			
Homework Tasks	☐ ☐ ☐ ☐	☐ ☐ ☐	☐ ☐ ☐ ☐
Additional Notes			

THURSDAY

FRIDAY

NOTES

REMINDERS

NEXT WEEK

DOODLES

MONDAY	TUESDAY	WEDNESDAY

To Pack/bring

Monday: ☐ ☐ ☐ ☐
Tuesday: ☐ ☐ ☐ ☐
Wednesday: ☐ ☐ ☐ ☐

Assignments Due

Monday: ☐ ☐ ☐ ☐
Tuesday: ☐ ☐ ☐ ☐
Wednesday: ☐ ☐ ☐ ☐

Class Notes

Homework Tasks

Monday: ☐ ☐ ☐ ☐
Tuesday: ☐ ☐ ☐ ☐
Wednesday: ☐ ☐ ☐ ☐

Additional Notes

THURSDAY

FRIDAY

NOTES

REMINDERS

NEXT WEEK

DOODLES

MONDAY	TUESDAY	WEDNESDAY

To Pack/bring

- [ ]
- [ ]
- [ ]
- [ ]

Assignments Due

- [ ]
- [ ]
- [ ]
- [ ]

Class Notes

Homework Tasks

- [ ]
- [ ]
- [ ]
- [ ]

Additional Notes

THURSDAY

FRIDAY

NOTES

REMINDERS

NEXT WEEK

DOODLES

	MONDAY	TUESDAY	WEDNESDAY
To Pack/bring	☐ ☐ ☐ ☐	☐ ☐ ☐ ☐	☐ ☐ ☐ ☐
Assignments Due	☐ ☐ ☐ ☐	☐ ☐ ☐ ☐	☐ ☐ ☐ ☐
Class Notes			
Homework Tasks	☐ ☐ ☐ ☐	☐ ☐ ☐ ☐	☐ ☐ ☐ ☐
Additional Notes			

THURSDAY

FRIDAY

NOTES

REMINDERS

NEXT WEEK

DOODLES

	MONDAY	TUESDAY	WEDNESDAY
To Pack/bring	☐ ☐ ☐ ☐	☐ ☐ ☐ ☐	☐ ☐ ☐ ☐
Assignments Due	☐ ☐ ☐ ☐	☐ ☐ ☐ ☐	☐ ☐ ☐ ☐
Class Notes			
Homework Tasks	☐ ☐ ☐ ☐	☐ ☐ ☐ ☐	☐ ☐ ☐ ☐
Additional Notes			

THURSDAY

FRIDAY

NOTES

REMINDERS

NEXT WEEK

DOODLES

	MONDAY	TUESDAY	WEDNESDAY
To Pack/bring	☐ ☐ ☐ ☐	☐ ☐ ☐ ☐	☐ ☐ ☐ ☐
Assignments Due	☐ ☐ ☐ ☐	☐ ☐ ☐ ☐	☐ ☐ ☐ ☐
Class Notes			
Homework Tasks	☐ ☐ ☐ ☐	☐ ☐ ☐ ☐	☐ ☐ ☐ ☐
Additional Notes			

THURSDAY

FRIDAY

NOTES

REMINDERS

NEXT WEEK

DOODLES

	MONDAY	TUESDAY	WEDNESDAY
To Pack/bring	☐ ☐ ☐ ☐	☐ ☐ ☐ ☐	☐ ☐ ☐ ☐
Assignments Due	☐ ☐ ☐ ☐	☐ ☐ ☐	☐ ☐ ☐
Class Notes			
Homework Tasks	☐ ☐ ☐ ☐	☐ ☐ ☐ ☐	☐ ☐ ☐ ☐
Additional Notes			

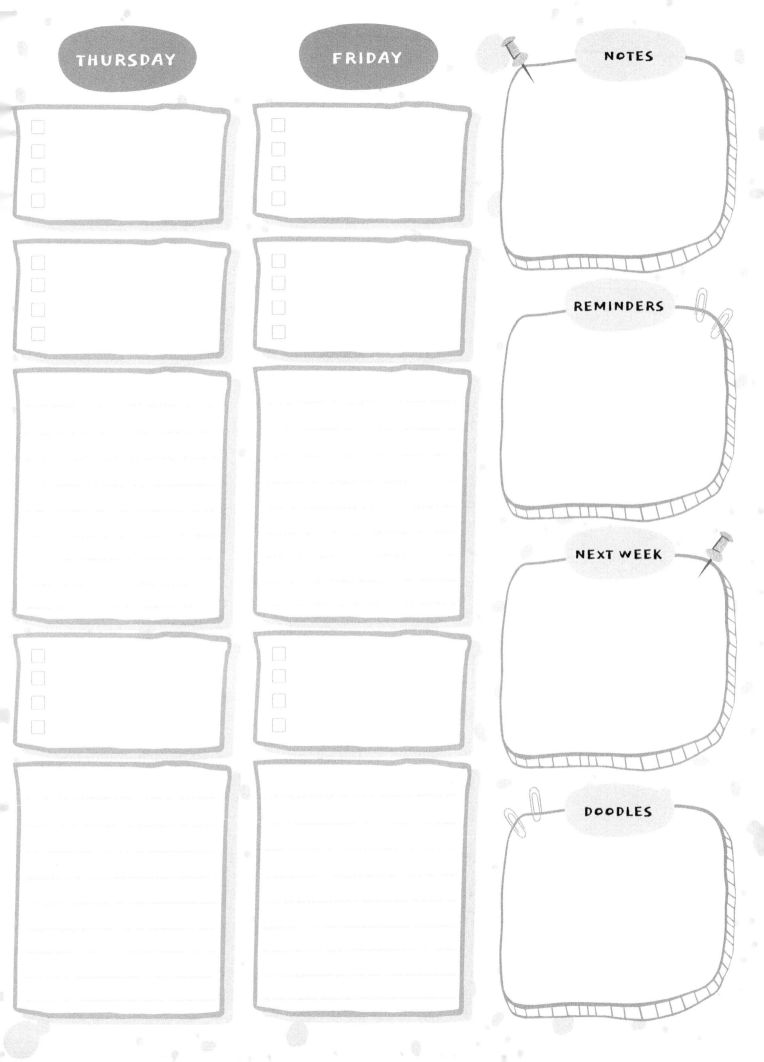

THURSDAY

FRIDAY

NOTES

REMINDERS

NEXT WEEK

DOODLES

MONDAY

TUESDAY

WEDNESDAY

To Pack/bring

- [ ]
- [ ]
- [ ]
- [ ]

Assignments Due

- [ ]
- [ ]
- [ ]
- [ ]

Class Notes

Homework Tasks

- [ ]
- [ ]
- [ ]
- [ ]

Additional Notes

THURSDAY

FRIDAY

NOTES

REMINDERS

NEXT WEEK

DOODLES

	MONDAY	TUESDAY	WEDNESDAY
To Pack/bring	☐ ☐ ☐ ☐	☐ ☐ ☐ ☐	☐ ☐ ☐ ☐
Assignments Due	☐ ☐ ☐ ☐	☐ ☐ ☐ ☐	☐ ☐ ☐ ☐
Class Notes			
Homework Tasks	☐ ☐ ☐ ☐	☐ ☐ ☐ ☐	☐ ☐ ☐ ☐
Additional Notes			

THURSDAY

FRIDAY

NOTES

REMINDERS

NEXT WEEK

DOODLES

	MONDAY	**TUESDAY**	**WEDNESDAY**
To Pack/bring	☐ ☐ ☐ ☐	☐ ☐ ☐ ☐	☐ ☐ ☐ ☐
Assignments Due	☐ ☐ ☐ ☐	☐ ☐ ☐ ☐	☐ ☐ ☐ ☐
Class Notes			
Homework Tasks	☐ ☐ ☐ ☐	☐ ☐ ☐ ☐	☐ ☐ ☐ ☐
Additional Notes			

THURSDAY

FRIDAY

NOTES

REMINDERS

NEXT WEEK

DOODLES

	MONDAY	**TUESDAY**	**WEDNESDAY**
To Pack/bring	☐ ☐ ☐ ☐	☐ ☐ ☐ ☐	☐ ☐ ☐ ☐
Assignments Due	☐ ☐ ☐ ☐	☐	☐ ☐ ☐ ☐
Class Notes			
Homework Tasks	☐ ☐ ☐ ☐	☐ ☐ ☐ ☐	☐ ☐ ☐ ☐
Additional Notes			

THURSDAY

FRIDAY

NOTES

REMINDERS

NEXT WEEK

DOODLES

	MONDAY	TUESDAY	WEDNESDAY
To pack/bring	☐ ☐ ☐ ☐	☐ ☐ ☐ ☐	☐ ☐ ☐ ☐
Assignments Due	☐ ☐ ☐ ☐	☐ ☐ ☐ ☐	☐ ☐ ☐ ☐
Class Notes			
Homework Tasks	☐ ☐ ☐ ☐	☐ ☐ ☐ ☐	☐ ☐ ☐ ☐
Additional Notes			

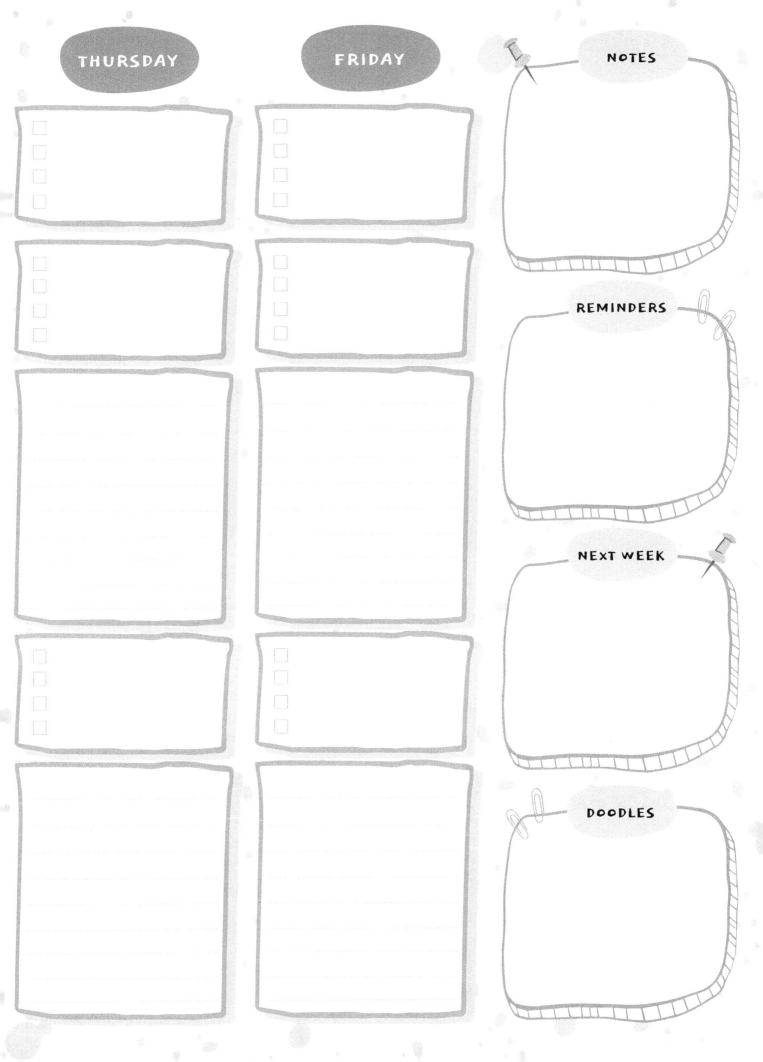

THURSDAY

FRIDAY

NOTES

REMINDERS

NEXT WEEK

DOODLES

	MONDAY	**TUESDAY**	**WEDNESDAY**
To Pack/bring	☐ ☐ ☐ ☐	☐ ☐ ☐ ☐	☐ ☐ ☐ ☐
Assignments Due	☐ ☐ ☐ ☐	☐ ☐ ☐ ☐	☐ ☐ ☐ ☐
Class Notes			
Homework Tasks	☐ ☐ ☐ ☐	☐ ☐ ☐ ☐	☐ ☐ ☐ ☐
Additional Notes			

THURSDAY

FRIDAY

NOTES

REMINDERS

NEXT WEEK

DOODLES

	MONDAY	TUESDAY	WEDNESDAY
To Pack/bring	☐ ☐ ☐ ☐	☐ ☐ ☐ ☐	☐ ☐ ☐ ☐
Assignments Due	☐ ☐ ☐ ☐	☐ ☐ ☐ ☐	☐ ☐ ☐ ☐
Class Notes			
Homework Tasks	☐ ☐ ☐ ☐	☐ ☐ ☐ ☐	☐ ☐ ☐ ☐
Additional Notes			

THURSDAY

FRIDAY

NOTES

REMINDERS

NEXT WEEK

DOODLES

WEEK	MONDAY	TUESDAY	WEDNESDAY
To Pack/bring	☐ ☐ ☐ ☐	☐ ☐ ☐ ☐	☐ ☐ ☐ ☐
Assignments Due	☐ ☐ ☐ ☐	☐	☐ ☐ ☐ ☐
Class Notes			
Homework Tasks	☐ ☐ ☐ ☐	☐ ☐ ☐ ☐	☐ ☐ ☐ ☐
Additional Notes			

THURSDAY

FRIDAY

NOTES

REMINDERS

NEXT WEEK

DOODLES

	MONDAY	TUESDAY	WEDNESDAY
To Pack/bring	☐ ☐ ☐ ☐	☐ ☐ ☐ ☐	☐ ☐ ☐ ☐
Assignments Due	☐ ☐ ☐ ☐	☐ ☐ ☐ ☐	☐ ☐ ☐ ☐
Class Notes			
Homework Tasks	☐ ☐ ☐ ☐	☐ ☐ ☐ ☐	☐ ☐ ☐ ☐
Additional Notes			

THURSDAY

FRIDAY

NOTES

REMINDERS

NEXT WEEK

DOODLES

	MONDAY	TUESDAY	WEDNESDAY
To Pack/bring	☐ ☐ ☐ ☐	☐ ☐ ☐ ☐	☐ ☐ ☐ ☐
Assignments Due	☐ ☐ ☐ ☐	☐ ☐ ☐	☐ ☐ ☐
Class Notes			
Homework Tasks	☐ ☐ ☐ ☐	☐ ☐ ☐ ☐	☐ ☐ ☐ ☐
Additional Notes			

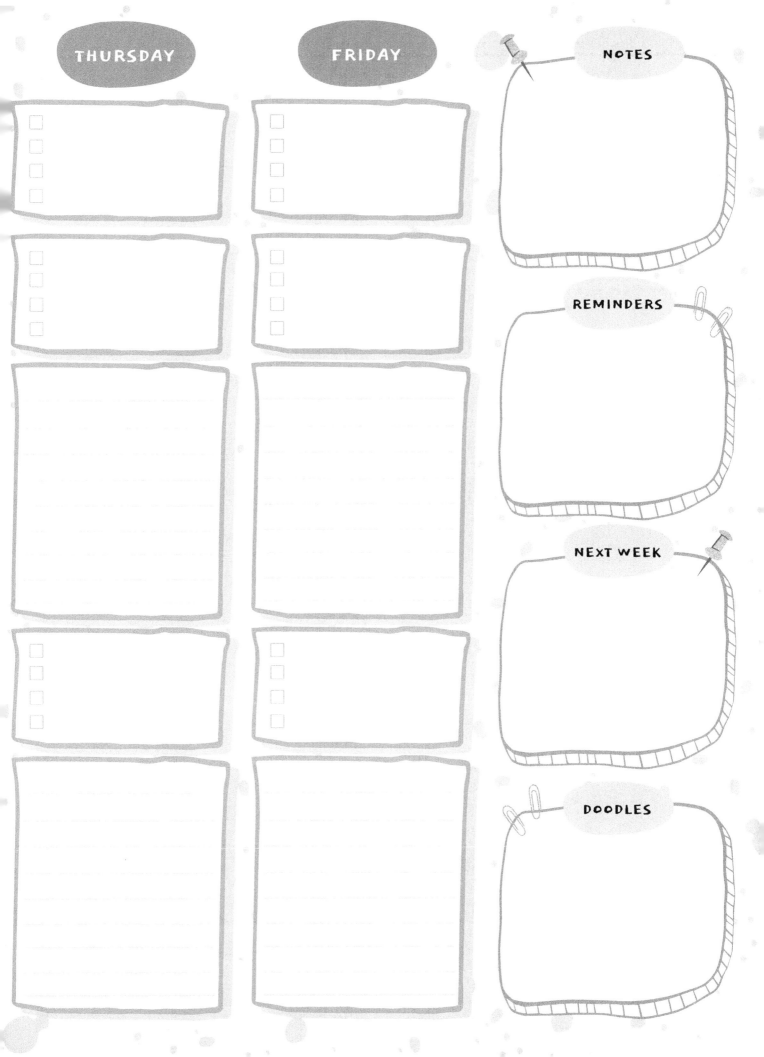

THURSDAY

FRIDAY

NOTES

REMINDERS

NEXT WEEK

DOODLES

	MONDAY	TUESDAY	WEDNESDAY
To pack/bring	☐ ☐ ☐ ☐	☐ ☐ ☐ ☐	☐ ☐ ☐ ☐
Assignments Due	☐ ☐ ☐ ☐	☐ ☐ ☐ ☐	☐ ☐ ☐ ☐
Class Notes			
Homework Tasks	☐ ☐ ☐ ☐	☐ ☐ ☐ ☐	☐ ☐ ☐ ☐
Additional Notes			

THURSDAY

FRIDAY

NOTES

REMINDERS

NEXT WEEK

DOODLES

	MONDAY	TUESDAY	WEDNESDAY
To Pack/bring	☐ ☐ ☐ ☐	☐ ☐ ☐ ☐	☐ ☐ ☐ ☐
Assignments Due	☐ ☐ ☐ ☐	☐ ☐ ☐ ☐	☐ ☐ ☐ ☐
Class Notes			
Homework Tasks	☐ ☐ ☐ ☐	☐ ☐ ☐ ☐	☐ ☐ ☐ ☐
Additional Notes			

THURSDAY

FRIDAY

NOTES

REMINDERS

NEXT WEEK

DOODLES

	MONDAY	TUESDAY	WEDNESDAY
To Pack/bring	☐ ☐ ☐ ☐	☐ ☐ ☐ ☐	☐ ☐ ☐ ☐
Assignments Due	☐ ☐ ☐ ☐	☐ ☐ ☐ ☐ ☐	☐ ☐ ☐ ☐
Class Notes			
Homework Tasks	☐ ☐ ☐ ☐	☐ ☐ ☐ ☐	☐ ☐ ☐ ☐
Additional Notes			

THURSDAY

FRIDAY

NOTES

REMINDERS

NEXT WEEK

DOODLES

	MONDAY	**TUESDAY**	**WEDNESDAY**
To Pack/bring	☐ ☐ ☐ ☐	☐ ☐ ☐ ☐	☐ ☐ ☐ ☐
Assignments Due	☐ ☐ ☐ ☐	☐ ☐ ☐	☐ ☐ ☐ ☐
Class Notes			
Homework Tasks	☐ ☐ ☐ ☐	☐ ☐ ☐ ☐	☐ ☐ ☐ ☐
Additional Notes			

THURSDAY

FRIDAY

NOTES

REMINDERS

NEXT WEEK

DOODLES

	MONDAY	TUESDAY	WEDNESDAY
To Pack/bring	☐ ☐ ☐ ☐	☐ ☐ ☐ ☐	☐ ☐ ☐ ☐
Assignments Due	☐ ☐ ☐ ☐	☐ ☐ ☐ ☐	☐ ☐ ☐ ☐
Class Notes			
Homework Tasks	☐ ☐ ☐ ☐	☐ ☐ ☐ ☐	☐ ☐ ☐ ☐
Additional Notes			

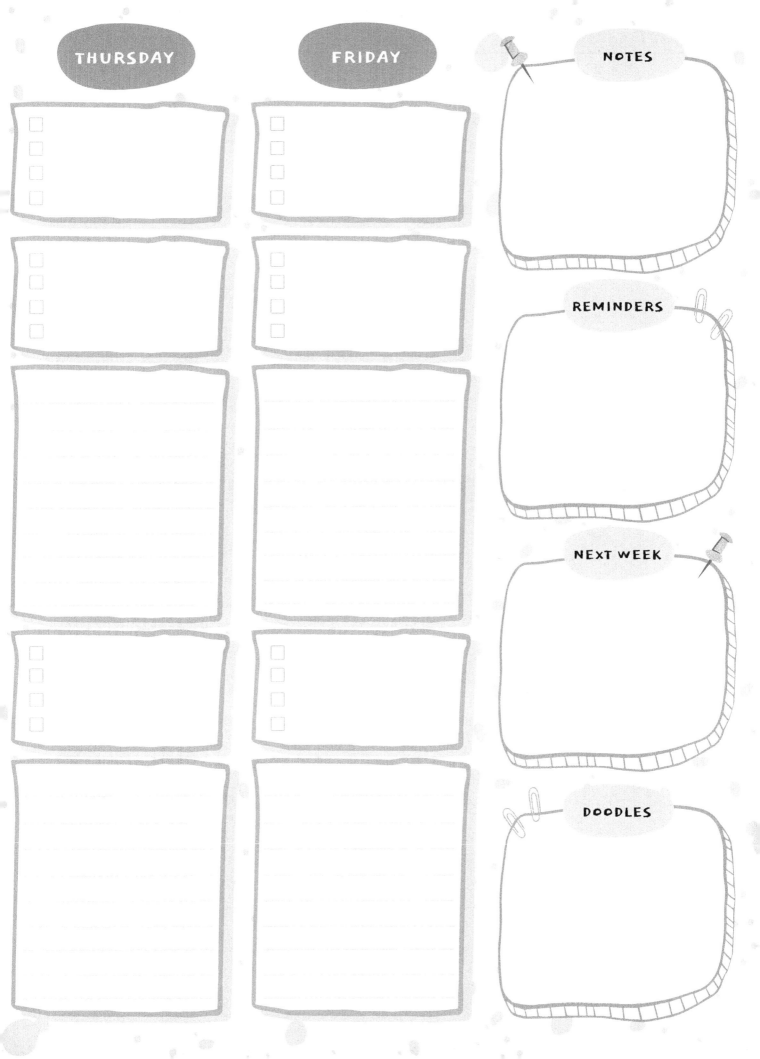

THURSDAY

FRIDAY

NOTES

REMINDERS

NEXT WEEK

DOODLES

	MONDAY	TUESDAY	WEDNESDAY
To Pack/bring	☐ ☐ ☐ ☐	☐ ☐ ☐ ☐	☐ ☐ ☐ ☐
Assignments Due	☐ ☐ ☐ ☐	☐ ☐ ☐ ☐	☐ ☐ ☐ ☐
Class Notes			
Homework Tasks	☐ ☐ ☐ ☐	☐ ☐ ☐ ☐	☐ ☐ ☐ ☐
Additional Notes			

THURSDAY

- [ ]
- [ ]
- [ ]
- [ ]

- [ ]
- [ ]
- [ ]
- [ ]

- [ ]
- [ ]
- [ ]
- [ ]

FRIDAY

- [ ]
- [ ]
- [ ]
- [ ]

- [ ]
- [ ]
- [ ]

- [ ]
- [ ]
- [ ]

NOTES

REMINDERS

NEXT WEEK

DOODLES

	MONDAY	TUESDAY	WEDNESDAY
To Pack/bring	☐ ☐ ☐ ☐	☐ ☐ ☐ ☐	☐ ☐ ☐ ☐
Assignments Due	☐ ☐ ☐ ☐	☐ ☐ ☐ ☐	☐ ☐ ☐ ☐
Class Notes			
Homework Tasks	☐ ☐ ☐ ☐	☐ ☐ ☐ ☐	☐ ☐ ☐ ☐
Additional Notes			

THURSDAY

FRIDAY

NOTES

REMINDERS

NEXT WEEK

DOODLES

MONDAY	TUESDAY	WEDNESDAY

To Pack/bring

☐	☐	☐
☐	☐	☐
☐	☐	☐
☐	☐	☐

Assignments Due

☐	☐	☐
☐	☐	☐
☐	☐	☐
☐	☐	☐

Class Notes

Homework Tasks

☐	☐	☐
☐	☐	☐
☐	☐	☐
☐	☐	☐

Additional Notes

THURSDAY

- ☐
- ☐
- ☐
- ☐

- ☐
- ☐
- ☐
- ☐

- ☐
- ☐
- ☐
- ☐

FRIDAY

- ☐
- ☐
- ☐
- ☐

- ☐
- ☐
- ☐
- ☐

- ☐
- ☐
- ☐

NOTES

REMINDERS

NEXT WEEK

DOODLES

	MONDAY	TUESDAY	WEDNESDAY
To Pack/bring	☐ ☐ ☐ ☐	☐ ☐ ☐ ☐	☐ ☐ ☐ ☐
Assignments Due	☐ ☐ ☐ ☐	☐ ☐ ☐ ☐	☐ ☐ ☐ ☐
Class Notes			
Homework Tasks	☐ ☐ ☐ ☐	☐ ☐ ☐ ☐	☐ ☐ ☐ ☐
Additional Notes			

THURSDAY

FRIDAY

NOTES

REMINDERS

NEXT WEEK

DOODLES

	MONDAY	TUESDAY	WEDNESDAY
To pack/bring	☐ ☐ ☐ ☐	☐ ☐ ☐ ☐	☐ ☐ ☐ ☐
Assignments Due	☐ ☐ ☐ ☐	☐ ☐ ☐ ☐	☐ ☐ ☐ ☐
Class Notes			
Homework Tasks	☐ ☐ ☐ ☐	☐ ☐ ☐ ☐	☐ ☐ ☐ ☐
Additional Notes			

THURSDAY

FRIDAY

NOTES

REMINDERS

NEXT WEEK

DOODLES

MONDAY	TUESDAY	WEDNESDAY

To Pack/bring

Assignments Due

Class Notes

Homework Tasks

Additional Notes

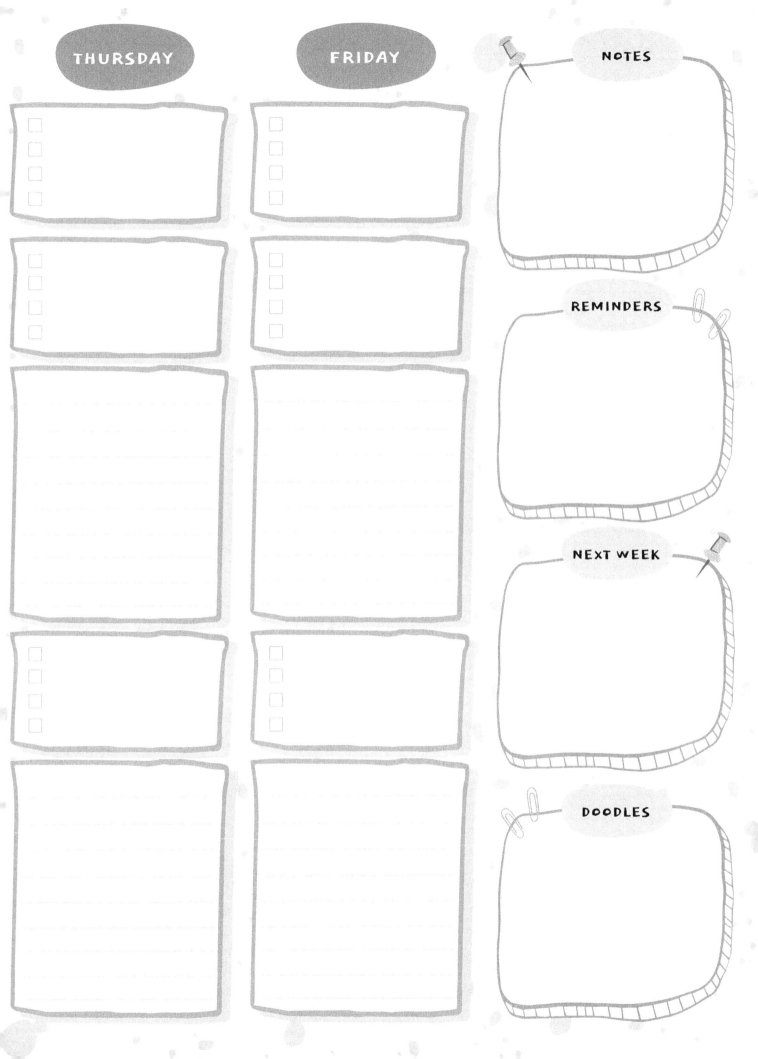

THURSDAY

FRIDAY

NOTES

REMINDERS

NEXT WEEK

DOODLES

	MONDAY	TUESDAY	WEDNESDAY
To Pack/bring	☐ ☐ ☐ ☐	☐ ☐ ☐ ☐	☐ ☐ ☐ ☐
Assignments Due	☐ ☐ ☐ ☐	☐ ☐ ☐	☐ ☐ ☐ ☐
Class Notes			
Homework Tasks	☐ ☐ ☐ ☐	☐ ☐ ☐ ☐	☐ ☐ ☐ ☐
Additional Notes			

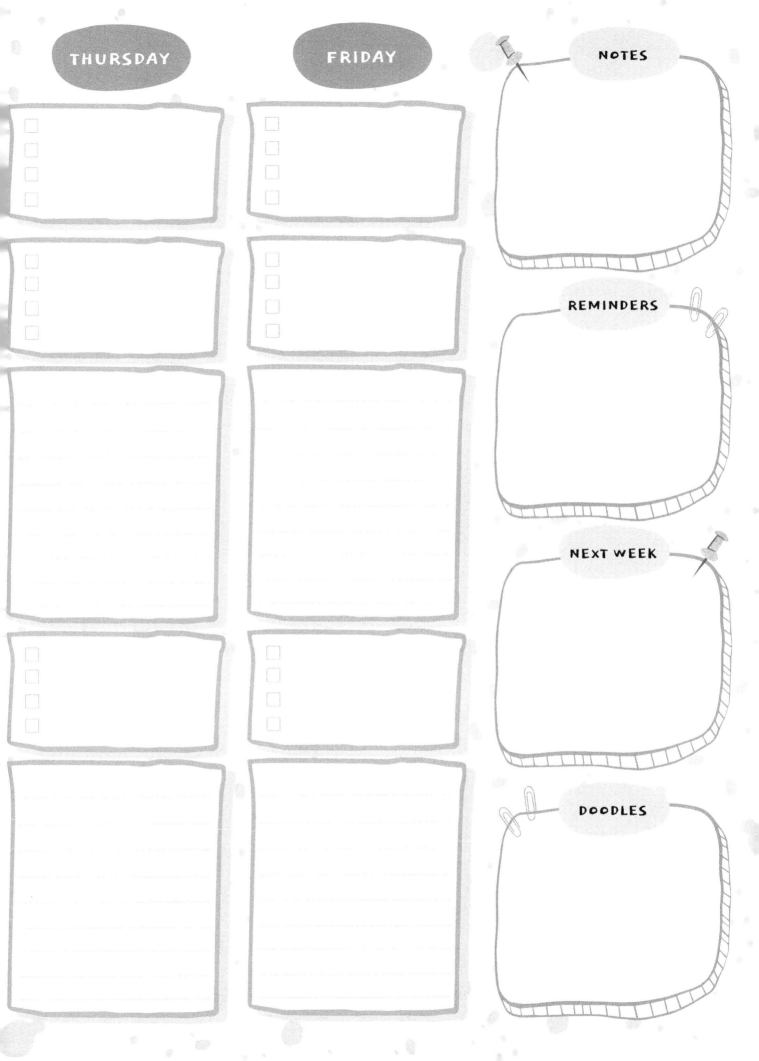

THURSDAY

FRIDAY

NOTES

REMINDERS

NEXT WEEK

DOODLES

	MONDAY	TUESDAY	WEDNESDAY
To Pack/bring	☐ ☐ ☐ ☐	☐ ☐ ☐ ☐	☐ ☐ ☐ ☐
Assignments Due	☐ ☐ ☐ ☐	☐ ☐ ☐ ☐	☐ ☐ ☐ ☐
Class Notes			
Homework Tasks	☐ ☐ ☐ ☐	☐ ☐ ☐ ☐	☐ ☐ ☐ ☐
Additional Notes			

WEEK

THURSDAY

FRIDAY

NOTES

REMINDERS

NEXT WEEK

DOODLES

	MONDAY	TUESDAY	WEDNESDAY
To Pack/bring	☐ ☐ ☐ ☐	☐ ☐ ☐ ☐	☐ ☐ ☐ ☐
Assignments Due	☐ ☐ ☐ ☐	☐ ☐ ☐ ☐	☐ ☐ ☐ ☐
Class Notes			
Homework Tasks	☐ ☐ ☐ ☐	☐ ☐ ☐ ☐	☐ ☐ ☐ ☐
Additional Notes			

THURSDAY

FRIDAY

NOTES

REMINDERS

NEXT WEEK

DOODLES

	MONDAY	TUESDAY	WEDNESDAY
To pack/bring	☐ ☐ ☐ ☐	☐ ☐ ☐ ☐	☐ ☐ ☐ ☐
Assignments Due	☐ ☐ ☐ ☐	☐ ☐ ☐ ☐	☐ ☐ ☐ ☐
Class Notes			
Homework Tasks	☐ ☐ ☐ ☐	☐ ☐ ☐ ☐	☐ ☐ ☐ ☐
Additional Notes			

THURSDAY

FRIDAY

NOTES

REMINDERS

NEXT WEEK

DOODLES

	MONDAY	TUESDAY	WEDNESDAY
To Pack/bring	☐ ☐ ☐ ☐	☐ ☐ ☐ ☐	☐ ☐ ☐ ☐
Assignments Due	☐ ☐ ☐ ☐	☐ ☐ ☐ ☐	☐ ☐ ☐ ☐
Class Notes			
Homework Tasks	☐ ☐ ☐ ☐	☐ ☐ ☐ ☐	☐ ☐ ☐ ☐
Additional Notes			

THURSDAY

FRIDAY

NOTES

REMINDERS

NEXT WEEK

DOODLES

	MONDAY	TUESDAY	WEDNESDAY
To pack/bring	☐ ☐ ☐ ☐	☐ ☐ ☐ ☐	☐ ☐ ☐ ☐
Assignments Due	☐ ☐ ☐ ☐	☐ ☐ ☐ ☐	☐ ☐ ☐ ☐
Class Notes			
Homework Tasks	☐ ☐ ☐ ☐	☐ ☐ ☐ ☐	☐ ☐ ☐ ☐
Additional Notes			

THURSDAY

- [ ]
- [ ]
- [ ]
- [ ]

FRIDAY

- [ ]
- [ ]
- [ ]
- [ ]

NOTES

REMINDERS

NEXT WEEK

DOODLES

	MONDAY	TUESDAY	WEDNESDAY
To Pack/bring	☐ ☐ ☐ ☐	☐ ☐ ☐ ☐	☐ ☐ ☐ ☐
Assignments Due	☐ ☐ ☐ ☐	☐ ☐ ☐	☐ ☐ ☐ ☐
Class Notes			
Homework Tasks	☐ ☐ ☐ ☐	☐ ☐ ☐ ☐	☐ ☐ ☐ ☐
Additional Notes			

THURSDAY

FRIDAY

NOTES

REMINDERS

NEXT WEEK

DOODLES

	MONDAY	TUESDAY	WEDNESDAY
To pack/bring	☐ ☐ ☐ ☐	☐ ☐ ☐ ☐	☐ ☐ ☐ ☐
Assignments Due	☐ ☐ ☐ ☐	☐ ☐ ☐	☐ ☐ ☐
Class Notes			
Homework Tasks	☐ ☐ ☐ ☐	☐ ☐ ☐ ☐	☐ ☐ ☐ ☐
Additional Notes			

THURSDAY

FRIDAY

NOTES

REMINDERS

NEXT WEEK

DOODLES

	MONDAY	TUESDAY	WEDNESDAY
To Pack/bring	☐ ☐ ☐ ☐	☐ ☐ ☐ ☐	☐ ☐ ☐ ☐
Assignments Due	☐ ☐ ☐ ☐	☐ ☐ ☐ ☐	☐ ☐ ☐
Class Notes			
Homework Tasks	☐ ☐ ☐ ☐	☐ ☐ ☐ ☐	☐ ☐ ☐ ☐
Additional Notes			

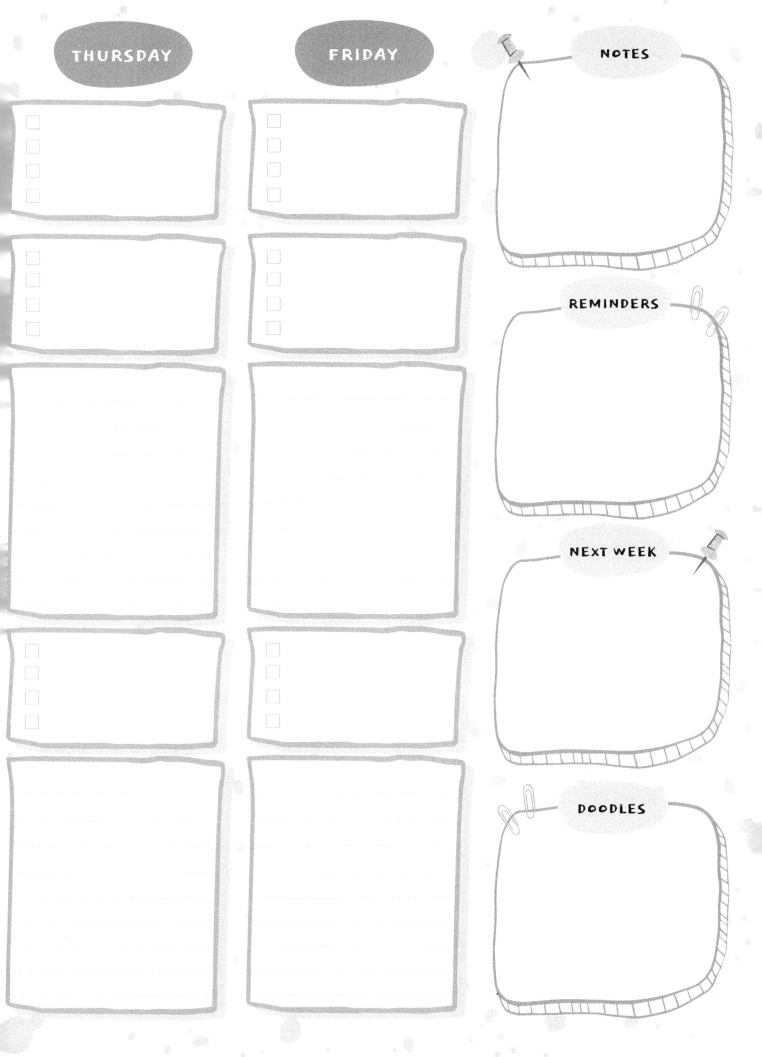

THURSDAY

FRIDAY

NOTES

REMINDERS

NEXT WEEK

DOODLES

	MONDAY	TUESDAY	WEDNESDAY
To Pack/bring	☐ ☐ ☐ ☐	☐ ☐ ☐ ☐	☐ ☐ ☐ ☐
Assignments Due	☐ ☐ ☐ ☐	☐ ☐ ☐ ☐	☐ ☐ ☐ ☐
Class Notes			
Homework Tasks	☐ ☐ ☐ ☐	☐ ☐ ☐ ☐	☐ ☐ ☐ ☐
Additional Notes			

THURSDAY

FRIDAY

NOTES

REMINDERS

NEXT WEEK

DOODLES

	MONDAY	TUESDAY	WEDNESDAY
To Pack/bring	☐ ☐ ☐ ☐	☐ ☐ ☐ ☐	☐ ☐ ☐ ☐
Assignments Due	☐ ☐ ☐ ☐	☐ ☐ ☐ ☐	☐ ☐ ☐ ☐
Class Notes			
Homework Tasks	☐ ☐ ☐ ☐	☐ ☐ ☐ ☐	☐ ☐ ☐ ☐
Additional Notes			

THURSDAY

FRIDAY

NOTES

REMINDERS

NEXT WEEK

DOODLES

	MONDAY	TUESDAY	WEDNESDAY
To Pack/bring			
Assignments Due			
Class Notes			
Homework Tasks			
Additional Notes			

THURSDAY

FRIDAY

NOTES

REMINDERS

NEXT WEEK

DOODLES

	MONDAY	TUESDAY	WEDNESDAY
To Pack/bring	☐ ☐ ☐ ☐	☐ ☐ ☐ ☐	☐ ☐ ☐ ☐
Assignments Due	☐ ☐ ☐ ☐	☐ ☐ ☐ ☐	☐ ☐ ☐ ☐
Class Notes			
Homework Tasks	☐ ☐ ☐ ☐	☐ ☐ ☐ ☐	☐ ☐ ☐ ☐
Additional Notes			

THURSDAY

FRIDAY

NOTES

REMINDERS

NEXT WEEK

DOODLES

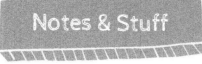

Notes & Stuff

Notes & Stuff

Notes & Stuff

Notes & Stuff

Notes & Stuff

Notes & Stuff

Notes & Stuff

Notes & Stuff

Notes & Stuff

Notes & Stuff

My Grades

Class \ Assignment														

My Grades

Class \ Assignment														

Made in the USA
Monee, IL
29 December 2020